Table of Contents

1 Introduction to Virtual Worlds 3
   1.1 The Metaverse and Self 5
   1.2 Virtual Reality's Potential 8

2 Gaming & Personal Growth 11
   2.1 Skill Development in Games 13
   2.2 Overcoming Challenges 15
   2.3 Social Interaction Online 18

3 Virtual Therapy & Wellbeing 21
   3.1 VR Exposure Therapy 24
   3.2 Mindfulness in Virtual Spaces 26
   3.3 Digital Support Networks 29
   3.4 Accessibility & Inclusivity 31
   3.5 Ethical Considerations 34

4 Avatar Identity & Self-Esteem 37
   4.1 Embodiment and Self-Perception 39
   4.2 Body Image in Virtual Worlds 42

5 Community & Connection Online 45
   5.1 Building Online Relationships 47
   5.2 Social Support & Belonging 50
   5.3 Combatting Online Isolation 53

Table of Contents

6 The Dark Side of Virtual Worlds 57
    6.1   Addiction & Virtual Reality 59
    6.2   Cyberbullying & Harassment 62
    6.3   Mental Health Risks 65
    6.4   Balancing Virtual & Real Life 67

7 Conclusion: Shaping the Future 71
    7.1   Future Trends in VR/AR 73
    7.2   Responsible Virtual World Design 76

1 Introduction to Virtual Worlds

Stepping into a virtual world feels different than scrolling through a social media feed. It's an immersive experience, a kind of digital inhabitation. You're not just observing; you're participating, interacting, becoming. This inherent difference is precisely what makes the metaverse such a powerful, yet potentially unpredictable, force in our lives. The implications for self-discovery are immense, a complex tapestry woven from technological advancements and deeply human needs.

Consider the act of creating an avatar. This seemingly simple process often reveals much more than a preference for certain colors or hairstyles. The choices we make – gender, race, physical attributes – reflect our conscious and unconscious desires, our aspirations, our anxieties. Do we create an avatar that mirrors our real-world self, or do we opt for a radical departure? The answer speaks volumes about our self-perception and our relationship with our own identity. This process of avatar creation, then, becomes a form of self-reflection and exploration, a journey of self-discovery in the pixelated landscape of the digital world.

Virtual reality (VR), unlike other digital platforms, offers a level of immersion that changes our experience of presence and interaction. The sensations are more potent; the connections, more immediate. In this fully-fledged virtual environment, we can confront fears, practice social skills, and explore new aspects of ourselves in a safe, controlled space. VR offers a unique pathway to personal growth, allowing us to develop strategies for dealing with anxiety or social situations in a risk-free environment.

However, the potential of VR extends far beyond therapeutic applications. The ability to step into different roles, to try on different identities without the constraints of the physical world, can be transformative. Imagine a shy individual becoming a confident leader in a virtual team-building exercise, or someone grappling with body image issues finding a sense of acceptance and self-love through a customized avatar. The possibilities for personal transformation are astonishing, almost limitless in their potential for positive change.

The key, of course, lies in understanding how our virtual selves interact with our real-world identities. Our experiences in virtual worlds are not isolated events; they influence our thoughts, feelings, and behaviors offline. A sense of accomplishment in a virtual environment can boost self-esteem, while negative experiences can have detrimental effects. Understanding the dynamics of this interplay—between virtual actions and real-world implications—is crucial for harnessing the transformative power of virtual worlds responsibly. Neglecting this crucial aspect can lead to potential pitfalls, making informed engagement essential.

Navigating this new landscape requires a nuanced approach. We need to be mindful of the potential for addiction, cyberbullying, and other negative consequences. Yet, simultaneously, we cannot dismiss the incredible opportunities these technologies offer for personal growth, community building, and therapeutic intervention. It is a delicate dance, a balance between embracing innovation and mitigating potential risks. The challenge lies in fostering a culture of responsible use, guided by empathy, awareness, and a commitment to the well-being of individuals engaging with these transformative technologies.

The introduction of the metaverse and the expansion of virtual reality technologies signify more than a technological leap; they represent a profound shift in how we experience ourselves and interact with the world around us. These spaces provide us with a canvas upon which we can paint new aspects of our selves, challenging preconceptions, and ultimately shaping a clearer image of who we are and who we aspire to be. Recognizing this potential, and actively working towards responsible use and development of virtual environments, is paramount to ensuring their benefits far outweigh their risks. This journey of self-discovery in the digital realm is a complex and evolving one, full of both incredible promise and inherent challenges. It is a path we must tread carefully, informed, and committed to responsible engagement. Our exploration of this digital frontier has only just begun, and the future unfolds before us, awaiting our mindful steps.

1.1 The Metaverse and Self

Exploring the metaverse often feels like stepping into a mirror reflecting a potential self. We craft avatars, meticulously choosing features and clothing, a digital reflection subtly shaped by our desires and insecurities. This process of creation, this act of building a virtual persona, is profoundly revealing. It's a window into our subconscious, a chance to experiment with identities we might never dare explore in

1 Introduction to Virtual Worlds

the real world. The choices we make—the boldness of an avatar's attire, the subtle nuances of their expressions—reveal much about our self-perception and our aspirations.

The immersive nature of the metaverse intensifies this self-reflection. In virtual reality, the line between observer and participant blurs. Our actions, our interactions, have immediate consequences within the virtual environment, forcing us to confront our strengths and weaknesses in a more direct, albeit simulated, way. Successes in virtual worlds can boost confidence, while failures, though not real-world consequential, offer valuable lessons in resilience and adaptability. This dynamic interplay between action and consequence is a powerful engine for self-discovery and personal growth.

However, the potential for self-deception also exists. We might craft avatars that embody idealized versions of ourselves, masking anxieties or insecurities. This is not inherently negative; it can be a valuable tool for self-exploration and experimentation. The key lies in recognizing the difference between escapism and genuine self-reflection. Becoming aware of how our avatar choices might be masking our true selves allows us to confront those underlying issues and begin to navigate them constructively.

The metaverse, therefore, presents both opportunities and challenges regarding self-perception. It offers a unique space for exploring different facets of our identity, testing boundaries, and experimenting with new behaviors. But, it also presents the risk of reinforcing negative self-images or escaping from real-world issues rather than confronting them. The crucial element is mindful engagement. Approaching the metaverse with self-awareness and a commitment to genuine self-reflection can transform it from a potential source of escapism into a powerful tool for personal transformation. By actively observing our own virtual behavior and its relation to our real-world self, we can derive significant insights into our strengths, weaknesses, and aspirations.

Furthermore, the social dynamics within the metaverse add another layer of complexity to self-discovery. Our interactions with others, the relationships we build, and the feedback we receive all impact our self-perception. The anonymity that some virtual spaces offer can be liberating, allowing individuals to express themselves without the fear of judgment that might be present in real-life interactions. Conversely, it can also foster behaviors that we wouldn't exhibit in the real world. Navigating this social landscape requires self-awareness and a careful consideration of how our actions impact both our virtual and real-world selves. Building healthy relationships in virtual spaces requires the same empathy, respect, and communication skills that are needed in real-life relationships.

Consider the impact of avatar customization on body image. In a virtual environment, we have the power to alter our physical appearance at will. This can be incredibly empowering for individuals who struggle with body image issues in the real world. Creating an avatar that reflects a desired physical form can foster a sense of self-acceptance and confidence. However, it's crucial to be aware of the potential for this ability to become a form of escapism, preventing the individual from addressing the underlying issues that cause body image dissatisfaction in the physical world. Therefore, a balanced approach—leveraging the positive aspects of avatar customization while maintaining awareness of the potential for avoidance—is paramount. The metaverse, with its unique blend of immersion and malleability, offers a powerful lens through which to examine and understand the self. It's a dynamic environment where self-perception is constantly being shaped and reshaped by our actions, interactions, and the choices we make in creating and inhabiting our virtual personas. By approaching it with intentionality and self-awareness, the metaverse can become a valuable tool for promoting personal growth and improving mental well-being. Ultimately, the journey of self-discovery in the metaverse, much like the journey of self-discovery in the real world, is an ongoing process of learning, adapting, and growing.

1.2 Virtual Reality's Potential

The immersive potential of virtual reality (VR) extends far beyond entertainment. Imagine stepping into a meticulously crafted environment, one tailored to your specific needs. This isn't science fiction; it's the rapidly evolving reality of therapeutic VR applications. Consider the possibilities for phobias: facing a fear of heights from the safety of a virtual skyscraper, or conquering social anxiety within a simulated social gathering. The controlled nature of these environments allows for gradual exposure, building confidence and reducing anxiety at a pace comfortable for the individual. Furthermore, the ability to manipulate variables within these simulated worlds allows therapists to fine-tune the experience for optimal therapeutic effect. Progress can be objectively measured and adjustments made accordingly, providing a level of precision impossible in traditional therapy settings.

For individuals struggling with PTSD, VR offers a unique pathway to healing. By carefully recreating traumatic scenarios within a safe virtual space, individuals can confront their memories under controlled conditions. This process, known as VR exposure therapy, facilitates emotional processing and desensitization, ultimately reducing the debilitating effects of trauma. The key lies in the ability to revisit and reprocess these experiences without the physical and emotional overwhelm associated with real-world flashbacks or memories. Unlike traditional exposure therapies, VR offers a greater degree of control and allows therapists to gradually increase the intensity of the simulated scenarios. This tailored approach makes the process more manageable and effective for patients.

Beyond therapeutic applications, VR offers considerable potential for personal growth. Consider the transformative power of mindfulness practices enhanced by VR. Imagine meditating in a serene virtual forest, the sounds of nature washing over you, or practicing mindful breathing exercises on a tranquil virtual beach. These immersive environments can significantly increase engagement and effectiveness, creating a profound sense of presence and tranquility. The visual and auditory stimulation provided by VR can enhance the meditative experience, making it easier to quiet the mind and focus on the present moment. This enhanced engagement translates to a deeper understanding of oneself and a more profound connection to the present. Many users report an increased ability to focus and manage stress after incorporating VR-enhanced mindfulness practices into their routines.

The capabilities extend beyond relaxation, too. We see increasingly sophisticated VR simulations used for skill development. Imagine learning a new language by engaging in realistic conversations with virtual characters in a foreign country, or improving public speaking skills by delivering a presentation to a virtual audience. The potential for personalized, adaptive learning experiences is significant, as VR allows for immediate feedback and repeated practice in a risk-free environment.

1 Introduction to Virtual Worlds

This personalized learning approach allows for increased engagement and retention compared to traditional methods. The immediate feedback provided in VR allows learners to identify weaknesses and adjust their strategies, leading to faster progress and improved skill mastery. The potential is truly expansive. The applications of VR in personal development are far-reaching, extending beyond therapy and skill training. The capacity to create tailored environments for self-discovery, personal growth, and emotional well-being is only now beginning to be fully realized. As the technology improves and becomes more accessible, we can expect to see even more innovative uses of VR for personal transformation. It holds a promise of helping people overcome personal challenges, develop new skills, and enhance their overall well-being in ways that were previously unimaginable. The future of self-improvement may well be pixelated, yet profoundly impactful. The exploration of this potential is not merely a technological advancement, but a significant step in expanding the possibilities for human growth and well-being. We stand at the threshold of a new era, where technology empowers personal transformation on an unprecedented scale.

2 Gaming & Personal Growth

Many find solace and growth in the seemingly frivolous world of video games. Consider the strategic depth of a real-time strategy game, demanding constant adaptation and resource management; these skills directly translate to professional environments, fostering critical thinking and problem-solving abilities far beyond the pixelated battlefield. The satisfaction of meticulously planning and executing a complex maneuver, whether it's conquering a virtual kingdom or navigating a particularly tricky project at work, provides a sense of accomplishment that fuels motivation and self-efficacy.

The intensely competitive nature of many games forces players to confront failure directly and repeatedly. Losing, frustrating as it may be, becomes a crucial learning experience. Analyzing mistakes, refining strategies, and persevering despite setbacks cultivates resilience, a vital trait for navigating life's inevitable challenges. This iterative process of failure, analysis, and improvement mirrors the growth mindset promoted in various self-improvement frameworks; the game itself becomes a personalized training ground for mental fortitude.

Beyond individual growth, online gaming fosters unexpected social connections. Team-based games necessitate collaboration, communication, and trust. Players learn to negotiate, compromise, and coordinate their actions to achieve a shared objective. These collaborative experiences build teamwork skills, improve communication effectiveness, and foster a sense of belonging within a virtual community. The shared struggle and ultimate triumph strengthen bonds, creating friendships that often extend beyond the confines of the game itself.

The immersive nature of modern games offers opportunities for exploration and self-discovery. Stepping into the shoes of a diverse range of characters, from fantasy heroes to historical figures, allows players to experiment with different personalities and perspectives, expanding their empathetic capabilities and challenging preconceived notions. Role-playing games, in particular, provide a safe space to explore complex moral dilemmas and develop a deeper understanding of human behavior, a journey far removed from the limitations of typical, real-world interactions.

However, this positive potential is not without caveats. The line between healthy engagement and detrimental addiction is often blurred, demanding self-awareness and responsible gaming habits. Setting boundaries, prioritizing real-world responsibilities, and maintaining a balanced lifestyle are crucial for reaping the benefits of gaming without succumbing to its potential drawbacks. Establishing dedicated playtime, incorporating breaks, and engaging in offline activities help maintain this critical equilibrium, preventing any negative spillover into other life domains.

Despite the inherent risks, the potential for personal growth within the gaming realm is undeniable. By cultivating self-awareness, establishing healthy boundaries, and approaching gaming with a conscious and mindful perspective, individuals can leverage the unique opportunities presented by virtual environments to enhance their cognitive abilities, bolster their resilience, and forge meaningful social connections. This requires careful reflection, and a willingness to actively monitor and manage one's engagement. The key lies in recognizing gaming not simply as entertainment, but as a potentially powerful tool for self-improvement, a dynamic platform for growth and development if utilized effectively and responsibly. The virtual world, in its vast and complex tapestry, presents a mirror reflecting not just our skills and limitations, but our potential for growth and transformation.

2.1 Skill Development in Games

Many games demand strategic thinking, requiring players to analyze situations, anticipate opponents' moves, and devise effective strategies to achieve their objectives. This isn't just about winning; it's about developing critical thinking skills applicable far beyond the game screen. Consider complex strategy games like Civilization or StarCraft; mastering these cultivates a remarkable ability to weigh multiple variables, assess risks, and adapt to changing circumstances, skills highly valuable in professional and personal life. The constant need for problem-solving inherent in gameplay sharpens cognitive abilities, building resilience and adaptability.

Team-based games, especially those requiring coordination and communication, foster collaboration and teamwork. Examples like Overwatch or League of Legends necessitate effective communication, shared decision-making, and the ability to work towards a common goal. These experiences directly translate to improved collaboration skills in real-world professional environments, improving communication, negotiation, and conflict resolution. Furthermore, understanding roles and responsibilities within a team, a common element in many games, teaches the value of individual contribution to overall success. Beyond the cognitive and collaborative benefits, many games encourage perseverance and resilience. Facing challenging levels or overcoming powerful opponents instills the importance of persistence, a crucial trait for personal and professional success. The ability to learn from setbacks, adjust strategies, and try again after defeat, is a valuable skill learned through repeated gameplay, directly combating feelings of discouragement and frustration. The iterative nature of gaming allows for continuous improvement and feedback, fostering a growth mindset that is vital for overcoming obstacles in any area of life.

Specific game genres offer unique skill-building opportunities. Action games often enhance reaction time and hand-eye coordination. Puzzle games boost problem-solving skills and logical thinking. Role-playing games, on the other hand, develop narrative understanding, empathy, and character development. The diversity of game genres provides a wide array of skill-building opportunities catering to various interests and learning styles. By consciously choosing games that align with desired skill development areas, individuals can actively shape their personal growth journey.

However, it's crucial to maintain a balanced approach. While gaming can significantly contribute to skill development, it should not replace other forms of learning and personal growth. A healthy balance between gaming and other activities is vital to avoid potential downsides such as neglecting real-world responsibilities or developing unhealthy gaming habits. Moderate, purposeful engagement with games provides a valuable complement to other life pursuits, fostering well-rounded personal development. Therefore, mindfulness and self-awareness of gaming habits is critical for harnessing its benefits without succumbing to potential drawbacks.

The transferable skills gained from gaming are numerous and surprisingly relevant to various aspects of life. Time management, crucial in balancing gameplay with other commitments, is a skill highly valued in most professional settings. Resource management, often a central theme in strategy games, translates directly to effective resource allocation and budgeting in everyday life. Even seemingly simple actions like navigating complex virtual environments can improve spatial reasoning abilities which may prove unexpectedly helpful. Recognizing these transferable skills and actively applying them outside the game world is fundamental to leveraging the benefits of gaming for personal growth.

Ultimately, the impact of gaming on skill development depends largely on the individual's approach. Conscious selection of games aligned with personal goals, coupled with mindful playtime management, is key to maximizing its potential for positive development. By understanding the diverse skill sets nurtured by different game genres, individuals can actively utilize gaming to enhance specific aspects of their capabilities. Harnessing the power of games as tools for personal growth requires both self-awareness and a strategic approach. This conscious engagement transforms simple entertainment into an avenue for meaningful development and self-improvement.

2.2 Overcoming Challenges

Many find themselves stymied by seemingly insurmountable obstacles within virtual gaming environments. Frustration mounts as complex puzzles remain unsolved, powerful opponents prove too formidable, and collaborative efforts falter. These experiences, though occurring within a digital space, mirror real-world challenges, offering a unique opportunity for personal growth and skill development. The key lies not in avoiding these difficulties, but in actively engaging with them, learning from setbacks, and celebrating even the smallest victories. This process strengthens resilience, sharpens problem-solving skills, and ultimately fosters a more adaptable and confident mindset that extends beyond the virtual realm.

Developing effective strategies for navigating these virtual hurdles often involves a systematic approach. Breaking down complex tasks into smaller, manageable steps is crucial. This approach prevents overwhelming feelings of inadequacy and allows for a sense of accomplishment with each milestone achieved. Analyzing past failures, identifying areas for improvement, and adjusting strategies accordingly are equally important. A simple record-keeping system, perhaps a digital journal tracking progress, successes, and learning points, can significantly enhance this self-reflective process. Remember, setbacks are inevitable, but the ability to learn from them is invaluable.

The social aspect of many virtual games presents further opportunities for overcoming challenges. Collaboration with others fosters teamwork, communication skills, and mutual support. Working together to conquer a difficult boss fight or complete a complex quest not only enhances in-game success but also builds valuable real-world interpersonal skills. Moreover, observing how others overcome challenges offers valuable insights and learning experiences. Sharing strategies, offering assistance, and receiving support in return fosters a sense of community and mutual respect, both inside and outside the game. It's

2.2 Overcoming Challenges

in these moments of shared struggle and eventual triumph that true personal growth flourishes.

Yet, overcoming challenges extends beyond the technical and social aspects of gameplay. Managing one's emotional responses to setbacks is vital. Frustration and disappointment are natural reactions to failure. However, allowing these emotions to consume one's experience can be detrimental to progress and enjoyment. Developing strategies for managing frustration, such as taking short breaks, changing tasks, or seeking support from others, is essential. This emotional regulation translates directly into improved real-world coping mechanisms, increasing one's resilience in the face of adversity. Mindfulness techniques, such as focusing on breathwork or simply observing one's feelings without judgment, can significantly assist in this process.

Finally, maintaining a healthy perspective is crucial. The virtual world, while immersive and engaging, should not define one's entire self-worth. Success and failure within the game are important but should be viewed within a broader context of life's experiences. Remembering that setbacks are opportunities for learning and that progress is not always linear is vital. Celebrating small victories and acknowledging personal growth, even in the face of persistent challenges, fosters a positive self-image and a sense of self-efficacy that extends beyond the pixelated landscapes of virtual environments. This broader perspective helps to maintain a balanced approach, ensuring that the virtual world complements, rather than dominates, one's overall well-being. The lessons learned in navigating virtual obstacles can indeed become powerful tools for navigating the complexities of real life. Embrace the challenges, learn from every experience, and watch your personal growth blossom.

2.3 Social Interaction Online

Online social interaction, a cornerstone of many virtual worlds, presents a unique blend of opportunities and challenges. While offering unparalleled access to diverse communities and fostering connections across geographical boundaries, it also necessitates a mindful approach to navigate its complexities successfully. Building positive relationships requires conscious effort and understanding of the nuances of online communication.

Unlike face-to-face interactions, online communication lacks the richness of nonverbal cues. This absence can easily lead to misinterpretations, escalating minor disagreements into significant conflicts. Therefore, clear and concise communication is paramount. Choosing words carefully and utilizing emoticons or other visual aids to convey tone can mitigate misunderstandings significantly. Active listening, paying close attention to what others are saying rather than formulating your reply, is crucial for building rapport and understanding perspectives. Remember, patience is key when navigating potential misunderstandings. Allowing time for clarification can prevent unnecessary conflict and foster more respectful dialogues.

The anonymity afforded by many online platforms can both empower and embolden users. While it can enable individuals to express themselves freely without fear of immediate judgment, this anonymity can also facilitate negative behaviors such as cyberbullying or harassment. Maintaining a respectful and courteous demeanor is crucial. Engaging in healthy debates, but always remembering that behind every screen is a real person, is vital for a positive online environment. Remember to actively disengage from toxic interactions. Reporting harmful behaviors to platform administrators can help ensure a safer space for everyone. Your well-being should never be compromised for the sake of online interactions.

Moreover, participating in online communities should enhance, not replace, real-world relationships. Maintaining a balance between virtual and real-life social connections is essential for overall well-being. Engaging in online communities can be a fantastic way to expand your social circle and make new friends, but real-world interactions offer a depth and richness that online communication often lacks. Remember that genuine connections require face-to-face interactions for complete understanding and meaningful growth.

Finding healthy online communities is also a vital aspect of positive online social interaction. Seek out groups and forums that align with your interests and values. Engage actively, contributing meaningfully to discussions and supporting fellow members. However, be discerning and cautious. Not all online communities are created equal, and some may harbor negative or harmful behaviors. Always prioritize your safety and mental wellbeing. Avoid communities that promote negativity or encourage harmful behaviors. Your online environment should be conducive to your personal growth and mental well-being. Choose your virtual spaces wisely.

Developing strong online relationships takes time and effort. Just like in real life, building trust and intimacy require genuine interaction and shared experiences. Be yourself, express your authentic self and be receptive to others' experiences. Embrace the opportunities for connection and support provided by online communities, but be aware of the inherent limitations of virtual interaction. Remember, strong relationships, both online and off, require mutual respect, active listening, and clear communication. Foster those elements, and you'll cultivate rich and rewarding online interactions.

The digital landscape, while offering amazing opportunities for social connection, presents a unique set of challenges. Being mindful of these challenges, actively working to promote positive interactions, and prioritizing your own well-being, are crucial for enjoying the benefits of online social interaction while mitigating potential risks. Remember, the virtual world is a reflection of the real world, and the principles of healthy relationships apply in both spaces. Maintain a healthy balance between your online and offline life. And finally, never underestimate the power of thoughtful communication and genuine engagement to build positive relationships in any environment.

3 Virtual Therapy & Wellbeing

Virtual reality (VR) offers a unique therapeutic landscape, particularly beneficial for conditions previously challenging to treat. Exposure therapy, for example, traditionally involves confronting real-life fears. VR provides a safe, controlled environment to gradually desensitize individuals to phobias like heights or social anxieties. By simulating these situations digitally, therapists can adjust the intensity and pacing, maximizing comfort and progress. The immersive nature of VR can lead to more effective results than traditional methods, making it a powerful tool in the therapist's arsenal.

Consider the transformative potential for individuals with PTSD. Recreating traumatic scenarios within a virtual environment, under the guidance of a trained professional, allows for controlled re-experiencing and processing of trauma. This controlled exposure, combined with cognitive behavioral techniques, can help patients reframe their negative memories and reduce the debilitating symptoms associated with PTSD. The virtual environment offers a layer of safety that is crucial for effective trauma processing, making it a crucial resource in modern trauma treatment.

3 Virtual Therapy & Wellbeing

Beyond exposure therapy, VR facilitates mindfulness practices in innovative ways. Imagine a calming virtual forest, meticulously crafted to soothe anxieties and promote relaxation. Guided meditation exercises, coupled with the immersive visuals and sounds of this virtual sanctuary, can deepen the meditative experience, offering a more engaging and accessible route to mindfulness than traditional techniques. This accessibility expands the reach of mindfulness practices to individuals who might find traditional methods challenging or unappealing.

The ability to connect with others from anywhere in the world is another significant advantage of virtual therapy. Digital support networks, formed within virtual therapeutic spaces, foster a sense of community and belonging among individuals facing similar challenges. Sharing experiences in a supportive environment combats the isolation often associated with mental health struggles, thereby promoting healing and reducing feelings of loneliness and stigma. These digital communities provide peer support and empathy in a unique and powerful way.

Furthermore, virtual therapy addresses issues of accessibility and inclusivity. Individuals with physical limitations or those residing in geographically isolated areas now have access to high-quality mental healthcare. The reduced cost of virtual sessions compared to in-person appointments lowers barriers, making therapy more financially accessible to a wider population. This is especially important in underserved communities lacking access to mental health professionals. The democratization of mental healthcare through virtual platforms is a powerful step forward.

However, ethical considerations are paramount. Data privacy, the potential for misuse of personal information, and the need for qualified therapists to oversee virtual sessions must be carefully addressed. Establishing clear guidelines, ensuring data security, and maintaining high professional standards are essential to prevent potential ethical breaches. The focus must remain on patient well-being and the responsible use of technology. The potential benefits of virtual therapy are immense, but this must be achieved with appropriate safeguards in place.

The evolving landscape of mental health necessitates ongoing assessment and innovation. The integration of VR, augmented reality (AR), and other advanced technologies into therapeutic practices offers the possibility of tailored, effective, and accessible interventions. Continuous research into the efficacy of virtual therapies, coupled with professional development for therapists in the use of these technologies, is essential to maximize the benefits of this rapidly evolving field. The future of mental health care incorporates the best of both worlds, bridging the gap between technological advancements and human connection to deliver comprehensive care.

Beyond the technological aspects, the success of virtual therapy hinges on the therapeutic relationship. Building trust and rapport with a virtual therapist is crucial for positive outcomes. Open communication, active listening, and empathetic engagement are just as important in the virtual world as they are in person. While technology plays a crucial role, the human element remains at the heart of effective therapy, whether delivered virtually or in a traditional setting. The quality of the therapeutic alliance translates irrespective of the medium.

Finally, remember that virtual therapy complements, rather than replaces, traditional methods. Some individuals may benefit more from in-person interaction, while others may find virtual therapy better suited to their needs. A balanced approach, utilizing both traditional and virtual methods where appropriate, can offer a comprehensive and personalized pathway to well-being. There is no one-size-fits-all approach to mental health; a holistic and flexible strategy is most effective. The integration of virtual therapy represents a significant evolution in the provision of mental healthcare, with far-reaching benefits for individuals worldwide.

3.1 VR Exposure Therapy

Virtual reality (VR) exposure therapy offers a groundbreaking approach to treating anxiety disorders. Unlike traditional exposure therapy, which involves facing real-life fears, VR allows for a controlled and gradual introduction to anxiety-provoking situations. This controlled environment minimizes the risk of overwhelming the patient while still providing effective therapeutic benefits. The immersive nature of VR significantly enhances the therapeutic experience, making it a powerful tool for confronting deeply rooted anxieties. Consider phobias: a patient afraid of flying can experience simulated flights, gradually increasing the intensity of the simulated turbulence or height. This controlled exposure allows for desensitization to fear triggers in a safe and supportive environment, something not readily achievable in real-world settings.

The process typically begins with a thorough assessment of the patient's specific anxieties and triggers. A tailored VR environment is then created, mirroring the patient's individual fears. This personalization is key – generic simulations are less effective than tailored environments that resonate directly with a patient's unique fears and experiences. For example, a person with social anxiety might participate in a virtual party scenario, gradually increasing the number of virtual people interacting with them. The therapist acts as a guide, providing support and encouragement throughout the process. This support is crucial in building the patient's confidence and reducing feelings of helplessness.

Many studies demonstrate VR exposure therapy's effectiveness. Research consistently shows significant reductions in anxiety symptoms for individuals treated with VR exposure therapy compared to control groups or those undergoing other treatment methods. However, the success of VR exposure therapy hinges on several crucial factors. The quality of the VR environment and the therapist's expertise are paramount. A poorly designed or technically flawed VR experience can hinder progress, even causing additional distress. Similarly, the therapist's ability to effectively manage the patient's emotional responses and tailor the therapeutic sessions is crucial for a positive outcome. The level of immersion, the therapist's support, and the patient's active participation are key factors in the success of the therapy.

The advantages of VR exposure therapy extend beyond its effectiveness. Compared to traditional exposure therapy, VR offers greater flexibility and accessibility. Patients can access therapy from the comfort of their homes, reducing travel costs and time constraints. This expanded accessibility makes VR exposure therapy particularly beneficial for individuals living in remote areas or with mobility limitations. Furthermore, VR allows for the safe and controlled simulation of situations that might be difficult or impossible to recreate in real life. Imagine the cost and practicality of repeatedly exposing a person with a fear of heights to actual heights versus utilizing a virtual representation.

Despite its numerous benefits, VR exposure therapy is not without its limitations. The cost of the equipment can be a barrier for some individuals, and not all anxiety disorders are equally responsive to this type of therapy. Additionally, the effectiveness of the therapy relies heavily on the quality of the VR experience and the therapist's expertise. Technical glitches or a lack of proper training can significantly impact the treatment's success. Furthermore, the immersive nature of VR can sometimes trigger feelings of discomfort or disorientation in certain individuals, necessitating careful monitoring and appropriate adaptations during the therapeutic process. The need for specialized equipment and skilled therapists limits its widespread implementation.

However, the field of VR exposure therapy is constantly evolving. Advancements in technology are leading to more sophisticated and realistic VR environments, further enhancing the therapeutic experience. Simultaneously, research continues to refine techniques and protocols, optimizing the therapy's efficacy across various anxiety disorders. Therefore, while limitations currently exist, ongoing developments in VR technology and therapeutic strategies promise to enhance VR exposure therapy's accessibility, effectiveness, and overall impact on mental well-being. We anticipate increasingly sophisticated software and hardware, coupled with improved therapeutic methods. The future holds significant promise for the widespread adoption of VR exposure therapy as a valuable tool in mental health care.

3.2 Mindfulness in Virtual Spaces

Cultivating mindfulness within virtual spaces presents a unique challenge and an exciting opportunity. Unlike traditional mindfulness practices, which often emphasize grounding in the physical world, vir-

3.2 Mindfulness in Virtual Spaces

tual environments demand a conscious shift in attention, a deliberate focusing on the present moment amidst the simulated reality. This requires a heightened awareness of both the internal experience – your thoughts, feelings, and sensations – and the external stimuli within the virtual world. The key lies in not becoming passively absorbed by the virtual experience, but in actively observing it.

Successfully applying mindfulness in virtual reality demands a proactive approach. It's not about simply escaping into a virtual world; rather, it's about bringing the principles of mindfulness to that environment. Begin by consciously choosing your virtual space, selecting environments that promote calm and reflection rather than those filled with overwhelming stimulation. A serene virtual landscape, a quiet virtual forest, or even a minimalist virtual room can serve as excellent starting points. Observe the details: the textures of virtual objects, the subtle movements of virtual foliage, the sounds of the virtual environment. Engage all your senses, but without judgment. Just notice.

Consider incorporating mindfulness practices you already utilize in your daily routine. Guided meditations, available through many VR apps, can be incredibly effective, offering a structured approach to focus and awareness within the virtual space. These guided meditations often lead users through body scans, breathing exercises, and visualizations, perfectly adaptable to the virtual setting. The integration of these techniques creates a powerful synergy, enhancing both the efficacy of the meditation and the immersion in the virtual environment. Remember, the goal is not to escape the virtual world, but to become more present within it, to witness the experience without emotional entanglement.

The ability to control your avatar presents a potent tool for mindful-

3 Virtual Therapy & Wellbeing

ness practice. Observe the movements of your avatar, paying attention to the subtle changes in posture and expression that reflect your internal state. Are your shoulders tense? Is your avatar's gait hurried or relaxed? These are reflections of your own physical and mental state. Recognizing these correlations can provide valuable insights into your present moment experience, fostering self-awareness. By actively engaging in the virtual experience through your avatar, you deepen the connection between your inner world and your interaction with the virtual one. The virtual realm, with its malleable characteristics, functions as a mirror, reflecting back not just your avatar's actions, but the nuances of your emotional landscape.

Moreover, the interactive nature of many virtual environments presents opportunities for mindful interaction with virtual entities and other users. Engaging in conversations, collaborating on tasks, or even simply observing other avatars in their virtual space can serve as fertile ground for practicing mindful awareness. Observe how your emotions respond to virtual interactions. Feel the empathy or frustration without judgment, simply observing the arising and passing of those feelings. The virtual world offers a unique laboratory for practicing interpersonal mindfulness, allowing you to explore emotional responses in a relatively low-stakes environment. This controlled environment facilitates the careful examination of one's own reactions, a crucial step towards emotional regulation and improved social interaction. The virtual world provides an environment to practice and refine these skills for real world application.

Ultimately, mindfulness in virtual spaces requires a thoughtful and intentional approach. It is not a passive activity; it's an active engagement with the virtual environment, combined with a conscious focus on the present moment. By intentionally selecting appropriate environments, adapting traditional mindfulness techniques, leveraging avatar interaction, and thoughtfully engaging with others, you can transform your virtual experiences into avenues for enhanced self-awareness, emotional regulation, and improved mental wellbeing. The virtual world, therefore, can become not a distraction from mindfulness but a valuable tool in its pursuit. Remember to integrate these practices gradually, starting with short sessions and gradually increasing the duration as your comfort and focus improve. The key is consistent and mindful participation, not perfect performance.

3.3 Digital Support Networks

Finding solace and support within digital spaces is becoming increasingly important. We're witnessing the rise of online communities offering unique forms of connection and camaraderie, transforming how people cope with challenges and build resilience. These digital support networks aren't simply about chatting online; they represent a profound shift in how we access and receive support, particularly for those who might struggle to find it elsewhere. The anonymity and accessibility offered can be truly transformative.
For individuals facing social anxiety or geographical isolation, the ability to connect with like-minded individuals across geographical barriers becomes a lifeline. Imagine someone battling a rare illness, feeling completely alone in their experience. A specialized online forum dedicated to that illness could provide a sense of belonging, a space to share experiences, fears, and hopes, fostering mutual understanding and validation that's often absent in offline environments. This shared experience transcends physical boundaries, creating a supportive com-

3 Virtual Therapy & Wellbeing

munity where no one feels alone in their struggles.

The structured nature of some online support groups can be particularly helpful. Many platforms use moderators to ensure constructive conversations, preventing the spread of misinformation or harmful interactions. This moderated approach provides a safer environment, allowing vulnerable individuals to engage more confidently. This careful management contributes to the overall health and wellbeing of the group, creating a positive and supportive atmosphere that encourages participation and engagement.

However, it's crucial to acknowledge the potential pitfalls. Online communities, while offering significant benefits, can also be breeding grounds for negativity and misinformation. Harmful behaviors like cyberbullying or the spread of false information can undermine the positive aspects of these communities. It's vital to be aware of these dangers and engage in these spaces mindfully. Choosing reputable platforms with clear moderation policies is a crucial step in mitigating these risks, ensuring a safe and supportive environment for all members.

Navigating the complexities of digital support networks requires a thoughtful approach. It's about finding the right balance between the benefits and potential drawbacks. This involves actively seeking out well-moderated platforms with established communities. Looking for platforms that emphasize respectful communication and clear guidelines is key. Prioritizing mental health and well-being requires carefully evaluating the impact of virtual interactions on your overall emotional health.

Moreover, building trust within these virtual spaces is paramount. It's a gradual process, often built through consistent engagement and thoughtful interactions. Sharing personal experiences, even if vulnerable, can foster stronger connections and deepen the sense of belonging. Reciprocity is key. Active listening, offering support to others, and contributing positively to group discussions strengthen both individual and collective well-being.

The anonymity provided by certain online platforms can be both a blessing and a curse. While it allows individuals to express themselves freely without fear of judgment, it can also lead to a lack of accountability. Therefore, maintaining a level of transparency and responsibility in one's online interactions is critical. Open communication is often essential for maintaining healthy relationships, both online and off.

Ultimately, digital support networks represent a powerful tool in our ongoing quest for personal well-being and growth. They offer unprecedented opportunities for connection and mutual support, transcending geographical boundaries and social barriers. However, responsible engagement and a mindful approach are crucial to harnessing their potential while mitigating potential risks. By understanding the nuances of these online spaces, we can leverage their power to build stronger, more resilient communities and improve our mental wellbeing. This conscious engagement fosters a healthy and enriching online experience, maximizing the benefits and minimizing the harm. The key lies in understanding the digital landscape and employing healthy strategies for engagement. Careful selection of platforms and active participation in constructive conversations are paramount.

3.4 Accessibility & Inclusivity

Creating truly accessible and inclusive virtual therapeutic spaces requires careful consideration beyond simply making the technology functional. We need to actively design for diversity, anticipating and addressing the unique needs of various user groups. This means moving beyond basic accessibility features like screen readers and keyboard navigation. True inclusivity necessitates a broader perspective, encompassing cognitive differences, physical disabilities, cultural backgrounds, and socioeconomic factors. For instance, consider the impact of varying levels of digital literacy. A user unfamiliar with VR technology might require extensive onboarding and tutorial support, preferably in multiple formats (video, text, audio) and languages. This should be incorporated seamlessly into the experience, rather than presented as a separate, potentially isolating, task.

The design of avatars themselves presents a critical opportunity to promote inclusivity. Offering a wide range of customizable options, beyond simply skin tone and hair style, is crucial. Think about the representation of disabilities. Users should be able to create avatars that reflect their own physical realities, promoting a sense of authentic self-representation. Furthermore, the design of virtual environments must account for sensory sensitivities. Some users might be overwhelmed by excessive visual stimulation or loud sounds. Therefore, settings that allow for the adjustment of brightness, contrast, and audio levels are essential for personalized experiences and comfort.

Language barriers represent another significant hurdle. While many VR applications currently rely on English, multilingual support is crucial for global reach. This goes beyond simply translating menus; interfaces must be culturally sensitive and accommodate diverse communication styles. Consider incorporating alternative input methods, such as voice recognition systems that support various dialects and accents. Subtitles and transcripts for all audio components must be accurate

3.4 Accessibility & Inclusivity

and accessible. Failure to address these linguistic needs will severely restrict the accessibility of VR therapy for a significant portion of the potential user base, limiting the impact of the technology.

Financial accessibility is often overlooked. The cost of VR equipment can be prohibitive for many individuals, especially those who may benefit most from virtual therapy. Exploring alternative models, such as community-based VR centers offering affordable access or subsidized programs for vulnerable populations, could dramatically broaden the reach of these therapeutic tools. Creative solutions such as partnerships with healthcare providers and insurance companies might also help alleviate financial barriers. Furthermore, developing VR therapy applications specifically designed to run on lower-spec hardware would greatly expand access to wider demographics, particularly in developing countries or underserved communities.

Beyond technological solutions, inclusivity extends to the attitudes and practices within the virtual therapeutic space itself. Therapists must receive specialized training in culturally sensitive practices and disability awareness. This training should emphasize the importance of creating a welcoming and judgment-free environment where all users feel comfortable expressing themselves authentically. This training should also include information about different learning styles, communication styles, cultural norms, and the specific challenges faced by people with various disabilities. By cultivating an understanding and appreciation for diversity, therapists create an environment where meaningful healing can occur.

Finally, continuous evaluation and feedback mechanisms are essential. Regularly soliciting feedback from diverse user groups ensures that accessibility and inclusivity remain at the forefront of development and improvement. This feedback should actively seek input from individuals with disabilities, people from diverse cultural backgrounds, and others who may have unique needs. The incorporation of user feedback throughout the design and development process is fundamental to creating a truly accessible and inclusive experience. Ignoring this crucial aspect would lead to a technology that excludes a huge range of individuals and limits the beneficial impact of virtual therapy. This ongoing process of improvement will enable the virtual therapeutic landscape to become truly representative and beneficial to all.

3.5 Ethical Considerations

The therapeutic potential of virtual reality is undeniable, offering innovative approaches to mental health treatment. However, this potential is inextricably linked to significant ethical considerations that demand careful attention. Ignoring these ethical complexities risks undermining the very benefits VR therapy aims to achieve, potentially causing harm instead of healing. We must prioritize patient well-being above all else.

Privacy is paramount. The sensitive nature of therapeutic interactions necessitates stringent data protection measures. VR therapy often involves collecting detailed personal information, including emotional responses and behavioral patterns within simulated environments. Robust anonymization techniques, secure data storage, and transparent consent protocols are essential to ensure patient confidentiality and prevent data breaches. Failing to prioritize this critical aspect jeopardizes trust and could have devastating consequences for those seeking help.

Informed consent is not a mere formality; it's the cornerstone of ethi-

3.5 Ethical Considerations

cal practice. Patients must have a comprehensive understanding of the VR therapy process, including its potential benefits, limitations, and associated risks. This understanding should extend beyond the technical aspects of the technology to encompass the potential impact on their mental and emotional state. Clinicians have a responsibility to engage in open and honest dialogue, ensuring patients feel empowered to make informed decisions regarding their treatment. Misrepresenting the process or pressuring individuals into participation undermines the very foundation of ethical care.

The therapeutic relationship, already complex in traditional settings, is further nuanced in virtual environments. The distance created by the technology can present both challenges and opportunities. While it might facilitate access for those geographically isolated, it can also impact the depth of connection and the therapeutic alliance. Clinicians must be acutely aware of these dynamics, actively working to cultivate trust and empathy within the virtual space. This requires adapting therapeutic techniques to suit the unique context of VR, fostering a sense of genuine connection despite the technological barrier.

Accessibility and inclusivity are vital, yet often overlooked, ethical concerns. VR technology, while increasingly affordable, remains inaccessible to many individuals due to cost, technological limitations, or lack of digital literacy. Efforts to bridge this digital divide are crucial to ensure equitable access to this innovative form of therapy. Moreover, the design of virtual environments should account for the diverse needs and abilities of patients, avoiding the creation of exclusionary spaces that reinforce existing inequalities. The goal is to create inclusive experiences that promote healing for all.

The potential for misuse of VR technology poses a significant ethical

3 Virtual Therapy & Wellbeing

challenge. The immersive nature of VR can be manipulated for exploitative purposes, creating environments that induce undue stress or reinforce harmful patterns. Ethical guidelines must be established to prevent the use of VR in ways that exacerbate mental health issues rather than alleviating them. Rigorous oversight and regulatory frameworks are crucial to prevent the exploitation of vulnerable individuals and uphold the integrity of therapeutic practice within virtual environments. We must ensure that VR remains a tool for healing, not a conduit for harm. The responsibility lies with all stakeholders to prevent its misuse. This requires constant vigilance and proactive measures to safeguard those seeking help.

Finally, ongoing research and ethical reflection are indispensable. The field of VR therapy is constantly evolving, presenting new ethical dilemmas as technology advances. Continuous evaluation of practices, alongside robust ethical review processes, is crucial to ensure the responsible and ethical application of VR in therapeutic settings. Open dialogue, collaboration between clinicians, researchers, and policymakers, is essential to navigate the evolving ethical landscape and ensure that VR therapy fulfills its promise of positive transformation without compromising the well-being of those it aims to serve. This collaborative approach is fundamental to establishing best practices that both protect patients and realize the potential of VR for mental health.

4 Avatar Identity & Self-Esteem

Creating your avatar is more than just choosing a hairstyle or outfit; it's a powerful act of self-expression, a digital reflection sculpted by your own hand. This process can profoundly impact your self-esteem, either boosting confidence or inadvertently triggering insecurities. Understanding this dynamic is key to harnessing the transformative potential of virtual worlds.

The freedom to design your virtual self offers unparalleled opportunities for self-exploration. Maybe you always wanted vibrant purple hair. Perhaps you secretly yearn for a physique you haven't yet achieved in real life. In the virtual realm, these desires are instantly attainable, providing a safe space for experimentation and self-discovery. This newfound freedom can translate into increased self-acceptance and a more positive self-image, empowering you to embrace aspects of yourself you might otherwise shy away from. The ability to visually represent aspects of your personality and identity that you perhaps can't manifest easily in the physical world opens doors to self-discovery that we often find difficult or impossible to access in our daily lives. This is a potent tool for personal growth.

4 Avatar Identity & Self-Esteem

Conversely, the very act of avatar creation can also exacerbate existing insecurities. The pressure to craft the "perfect" virtual self can be surprisingly intense. Spending hours agonizing over minute details can become a counterproductive cycle, leading to feelings of inadequacy and dissatisfaction. Comparing your avatar to others' meticulously crafted digital personas can fuel social comparison, a known driver of low self-esteem. This is particularly relevant for those already struggling with body image issues in the real world; virtual worlds offer a chance to escape these issues, but also provide a stage for them to manifest in potentially damaging ways. The pressure of conforming to certain standards of beauty and perfection is omnipresent in many online virtual communities. As such, it's crucial to remember that the virtual world should be a place of self-exploration and not a competitive arena of aesthetic perfection.

Therefore, a mindful approach is crucial. Rather than focusing on creating an unattainable ideal, concentrate on designing an avatar that genuinely reflects your personality and preferences. Embrace imperfections, and view your avatar as a work in progress, just like your real-life self. Experiment with different styles, don't be afraid to try things out and see what feels authentic. The process itself is an exercise in self-acceptance and learning. Consider this: your avatar is not a mask to hide behind, but a tool to explore different facets of your identity. Think of it as a form of creative self-expression, akin to writing poetry or painting. If you feel that you're spending too much time trying to craft the 'perfect' avatar, step back. Remember that your self-worth isn't determined by the aesthetics of your virtual representation. Furthermore, engaging with diverse online communities can positively influence self-perception. Witnessing a variety of avatars and interacting with individuals who embrace their unique digital identities can broaden your perspective and challenge preconceived notions about beauty and self-worth. Surrounding yourself with supportive and inclusive communities can foster a sense of belonging, reducing feelings of isolation and increasing self-confidence. However, it's crucial to be selective in the communities you join, avoiding those that perpetuate unrealistic beauty standards or promote negativity. Prioritize spaces that emphasize genuine connection and mutual respect. Remember that your real-life connections and support systems should always be your anchor.

Ultimately, the relationship between avatar identity and self-esteem is complex and deeply personal. While virtual worlds offer unique opportunities for self-discovery and positive self-perception, they also present potential pitfalls. By approaching avatar creation with intentionality, self-compassion, and a focus on authenticity, you can harness the positive power of these digital spaces to foster a stronger sense of self and improve your overall well-being. Remember to regularly check in with yourself, recognizing that your avatar is a representation of you, not the definition of you. The key lies in using this tool for self-growth, not self-criticism. It's about using the virtual environment as an experimental space, learning from both successes and shortcomings, and using these lessons to build a more positive sense of self.

4.1 Embodiment and Self-Perception

The way we perceive ourselves is profoundly intertwined with how we experience our bodies. This is true in the physical world, but it takes on a new dimension in virtual environments. In virtual reality, we inhabit an avatar, a digital representation that acts as a kind of second skin.

4 Avatar Identity & Self-Esteem

This avatar's appearance, capabilities, and interactions shape our self-perception in unexpected ways. Consider the meticulous customization available in many games: hair color, clothing style, even physical proportions can all be tweaked, leading to a tangible sense of control and self-expression that may be absent from real life.

This ability to mold our virtual selves offers a powerful tool for self-discovery and exploration. Imagine someone struggling with body image issues. In a virtual world, they might experiment with different avatars, gradually building confidence as they navigate interactions with a positive virtual reflection. This iterative process of self-creation can be incredibly therapeutic, allowing for experimentation without the social anxieties often associated with self-presentation in the physical world. However, the line between therapeutic exploration and escapism can be blurred.

The very act of inhabiting an avatar – embodied cognition, as researchers call it – suggests that our minds don't entirely separate the virtual from the real. Studies show that players often mirror their avatar's behavior, adapting their posture and even their emotional responses to fit the digital persona. This isn't just about role-playing; it's a deeper integration where the virtual experience influences our understanding of ourselves. We're not simply observing our avatar; we're feeling what it feels like to be it.

Conversely, negative experiences within the virtual world can significantly impact self-perception. Imagine experiencing repeated cyberbullying or social exclusion within a game. The impact isn't limited to the virtual sphere; this negativity can seep into real-life interactions, affecting self-esteem and confidence. The feeling of rejection amplified by the intense sense of presence in VR can create a powerful, and po-

4.1 Embodiment and Self-Perception

tentially damaging, feedback loop. Therefore, fostering a supportive and inclusive virtual community is crucial to mitigating these risks. Positive interactions can reinforce a healthy self-image; negative experiences can erode it.

But the link between avatar and self isn't always straightforward. The level of identification varies greatly among individuals and depends on the context. Someone playing a competitive first-person shooter might view their avatar as a tool, a means to an end, with less personal identification than someone designing a personalized avatar in a social VR space, crafting a meticulous virtual reflection. The implications are therefore nuanced; the positive effects of embodiment are not guaranteed, and potential harm is a real concern needing careful consideration.

Consider, for instance, the potential for virtual worlds to exacerbate existing mental health challenges. Individuals who already struggle with body dysmorphia could find themselves caught in a cycle of dissatisfaction, constantly tweaking their avatar to an unattainable ideal. This continuous striving for perfection in a virtual space can mirror and potentially worsen pre-existing insecurities. Similarly, individuals suffering from social anxiety might find their anxieties reflected and even amplified in the virtual environment, leading to avoidance and further isolation. The digital world is a mirror, reflecting our real-world selves and often magnifying both our strengths and our vulnerabilities.

For beginners venturing into these virtual landscapes, it's vital to approach self-creation mindfully. Experimentation is encouraged, but so is self-awareness. Recognize that the virtual world is a tool, not a replacement for real-life connections and experiences. Maintaining a healthy balance between virtual engagement and real-world activities is crucial. Seek out supportive online communities, prioritize positive interactions, and remember that your avatar is not a replacement for your real self – it's an extension, an exploration, a potential catalyst for personal growth, but ultimately, only one aspect of your identity. The key to navigating these pixelated pathways effectively is mindful engagement and self-awareness.

4.2 Body Image in Virtual Worlds

Unlike the carefully curated photos in magazines or the heavily filtered images on social media, virtual worlds offer a unique space to explore body image. You have the power to craft an avatar, a digital representation of yourself, from the ground up. This unprecedented level of control can be both liberating and challenging, depending on how you approach it. For some, it's a chance to escape the constraints of physical appearance, to experiment with different styles and identities without fear of judgment. Others might find themselves inadvertently mirroring their real-world insecurities, projecting anxieties and self-criticism onto their virtual selves.

The process of avatar creation itself is a powerful tool for self-reflection. Think about the choices you make: Do you meticulously sculpt your avatar's features to match your own, seeking a perfect digital mirror image? Or do you embrace the opportunity for transformation, crafting an avatar that embodies ideals, aspirations, or even stark contrasts to your real-life persona? These decisions, seemingly trivial at first glance, reveal much about your relationship with your body and your self-perception. Consider whether your choice reflects a desire for acceptance, a need for validation, or a longing for something different.

The social dynamics within virtual worlds also significantly influence

4.2 Body Image in Virtual Worlds

body image. While you might encounter a diverse range of avatars, interactions still often revolve around visual cues. The way others react to your avatar, both positive and negative, can significantly impact your own self-esteem. It's a complex interplay; the virtual world reflects and magnifies the complexities of real-world social interactions, where judgments based on appearance are, sadly, often pervasive. Remember that the actions and opinions of others within these digital environments do not define your worth. Your inherent value transcends any virtual representation.

It's crucial to understand that your virtual appearance doesn't define your real-world identity. The avatar is a tool, a customizable representation; it's not an extension of your inherent self-worth. Creating an avatar that adheres strictly to unrealistic beauty standards can reinforce negative body image, creating a vicious cycle of dissatisfaction. Conversely, using this malleable medium to experiment, to step outside of societal norms and explore different aesthetics, can be a liberating experience. The key is mindful creation and intentional interaction. Research indicates that spending excessive time focusing on perfect avatar aesthetics can negatively impact mental health. Studies have shown a correlation between increased time spent on highly customizable virtual platforms and increased body dissatisfaction in some users, particularly those already struggling with body image issues in the real world. This highlights the importance of maintaining a balanced approach – using virtual environments for creative expression and social connection, but not allowing them to become a source of undue stress or anxiety.

So how can you navigate these virtual landscapes in a healthy way? Firstly, be mindful of the messages you're internalizing. Question the

4 Avatar Identity & Self-Esteem

societal beauty standards that might be subtly influencing your avatar design choices. Secondly, remember that your avatar's appearance is a choice, and you can always adjust it. It is a fluid construct, not a fixed identity. Finally, focus on engaging in positive and meaningful interactions within the virtual world. Connect with others based on shared interests and values, rather than solely on appearance. Your self-worth should always be grounded in your experiences and qualities as a person, irrespective of your avatar's digital form.

The virtual world, like the real world, reflects a diverse tapestry of bodies and experiences. Embrace the opportunity to explore and express your individuality, but remember that true self-acceptance stems from a deeper understanding of oneself beyond superficial aesthetics. The ability to shape and reshape your avatar offers a chance for experimentation, self-discovery, and empowerment, but it's vital to approach this opportunity with intentionality and self-awareness. Never forget the real-world implications of your virtual actions and self-perception. Your self-worth is inherent and unconditional, a truth that transcends any digital realm.

5 Community & Connection Online

Finding genuine connection in a pixelated world isn't about escaping reality; it's about enriching it. Many initially seek virtual communities for gaming or specific interests, quickly discovering a surprising depth of connection. Shared experiences, whether a thrilling raid in an MMORPG or a collaborative project in a virtual workspace, foster bonds that transcend the screen. These connections can be surprisingly profound, offering support, camaraderie, and a sense of belonging that mirrors, and sometimes surpasses, real-world relationships.

Building meaningful online relationships requires intentionality, much like cultivating friendships offline. Active participation, consistent engagement, and genuine interest in others are key. Don't just lurk; contribute to discussions, offer help, and actively listen. Remember that building trust takes time, and online relationships, like any relationship, require nurturing. Authenticity is crucial; presenting a false persona will ultimately hinder genuine connection. Embrace vulnerability, but always prioritize your safety and well-being.

Social support, a cornerstone of mental well-being, finds fertile ground in online communities. Feeling a sense of belonging, knowing you're

5 Community & Connection Online

part of something larger than yourself, is powerful. Online communities provide this in many ways, from offering advice and encouragement to simply providing a safe space to share experiences and feelings. This feeling of acceptance can be especially valuable for individuals who struggle with social anxiety or isolation in their offline lives, offering a gentler, more controlled environment to develop social skills and build confidence.

Combating online isolation requires proactive steps. While the allure of virtual worlds can be isolating in itself if not approached thoughtfully, they also offer powerful tools to combat it. Actively seek out communities that align with your interests. Engage in activities that require collaboration and interaction. Join online groups related to hobbies, professional fields, or shared passions. Don't be afraid to reach out and initiate conversations. Remember, initiating contact is often half the battle, and the rewards of connecting with like-minded individuals can be significant.

The anonymity afforded by the internet can be a double-edged sword. While it allows individuals to express themselves freely and explore different facets of their personality without the fear of judgment often present in face-to-face interactions, it also presents challenges. Maintaining a healthy balance between online and offline life is crucial. Over-reliance on online communities can lead to feelings of detachment from the real world and impact real-life relationships. Establishing healthy boundaries is essential; setting aside dedicated time for offline activities and prioritizing in-person connections prevents virtual worlds from eclipsing real-life experiences. Remember that meaningful relationships are cultivated through both virtual and physical interactions.

Effective communication is paramount in navigating online relationships. Misunderstandings can easily arise due to the absence of nonverbal cues, so clarity and careful word choice are essential. Active listening is crucial – truly hearing what others say and responding thoughtfully builds trust and strengthens bonds. Be mindful of your tone and language, remembering that sarcasm and humor can be easily misinterpreted online. Practicing empathy, putting yourself in others' shoes, greatly improves online interactions. When conflict arises, address it directly but respectfully; seek resolution rather than escalation. Virtual worlds offer an incredible opportunity to forge deep and meaningful connections. However, recognizing and managing potential pitfalls is equally important. Developing healthy online habits and establishing clear boundaries is crucial for fostering positive relationships. While the allure of instant connection is undeniable, genuine connection takes time and effort, both online and offline. Remember to prioritize authenticity, embrace vulnerability, and cultivate both online and offline relationships for a truly balanced and enriching life. The key is to integrate your online experiences thoughtfully into your life, leveraging their benefits without allowing them to overshadow the richness of real-world connections.

5.1 Building Online Relationships

Cultivating meaningful connections online requires a nuanced approach, moving beyond superficial interactions to build genuine relationships. It's not simply about accumulating friends; it's about fostering a sense of belonging and mutual support within a digital community. This necessitates a conscious effort to engage authentically and build trust. Remember, the virtual world, despite its pixelated nature,

5 Community & Connection Online

reflects the complexities of human interaction.

Unlike fleeting social media encounters, deeper online relationships thrive on shared interests and consistent interaction. Joining online communities centered around your passions—whether it's a book club, a gaming guild, or a professional networking group—provides fertile ground for meaningful connections. Active participation is key; contribute meaningfully to discussions, share your expertise, and offer support to others. This reciprocal exchange is the foundation of lasting bonds.

Finding common ground is crucial. Engage in conversations that go beyond surface-level pleasantries. Share your thoughts, perspectives, and experiences, being mindful of vulnerability and reciprocation. Listen actively to others, demonstrating empathy and understanding. Remember, genuine connection hinges on mutual respect and understanding, irrespective of the digital medium.

Building trust requires consistent reliability and transparency. Be true to yourself online; avoid projecting a fabricated persona. Follow through on your commitments, respond promptly to messages, and be honest in your interactions. These actions cultivate a sense of security and reliability, vital for building any strong relationship, virtual or otherwise.

Navigating the potential pitfalls of online interactions is crucial. Be aware of the risks associated with sharing personal information online, prioritizing your privacy and security. Avoid disclosing overly sensitive details prematurely; build trust gradually. Maintain healthy boundaries, recognizing that online relationships should complement, not replace, real-world connections. Learn to identify and report harmful behaviors, protecting yourself and others within your online com-

5.1 Building Online Relationships

munity.

The virtual world offers a unique opportunity to connect with individuals across geographical boundaries. Embrace this diversity, celebrating the richness of different cultures and perspectives. However, always be mindful of cultural nuances and communication styles, avoiding misunderstandings and potential offense. Remember that communication can sometimes be misinterpreted in a virtual setting.

Remember, online relationships, much like those in the real world, require nurturing and maintenance. Regular communication, shared experiences, and mutual support are essential for sustaining these connections. Schedule virtual hangouts, participate in group activities, and check in with your online friends regularly. Just as in face-to-face relationships, consistent effort is key to maintaining the bond.

Maintaining a healthy balance between your online and offline life is crucial. While online communities provide invaluable support and connection, it's essential to avoid becoming overly reliant on them. Prioritize real-world relationships and activities, ensuring a well-rounded life that integrates both virtual and physical experiences. This prevents the virtual world from overshadowing your offline well-being.

Self-awareness is paramount. Understand your own online communication style, being mindful of how your words and actions might be perceived by others. Reflect on your interactions, identifying areas for improvement and actively working on enhancing your communication skills. Self-reflection allows you to build healthier, more fulfilling online relationships.

Ultimately, building fulfilling online relationships mirrors the process in the real world: it demands authenticity, vulnerability, and consistent effort. Embrace the unique opportunities afforded by virtual environments, while remaining mindful of potential challenges. By cultivating genuine connections and navigating the digital landscape wisely, you can foster a vibrant and supportive online community that enriches your life. Remember, the pixels may separate you geographically, but genuine human connection transcends the digital divide. Focus on building relationships founded on trust, mutual respect, and shared experiences, allowing for the development of lasting and supportive online friendships.

5.2 Social Support & Belonging

Finding solace and connection within the digital realm isn't always straightforward. While virtual worlds offer unprecedented opportunities for social interaction, navigating the complexities of online relationships requires careful consideration and a proactive approach. Building genuine connections, however, is possible and deeply rewarding.

For many, the anonymity offered by avatars can initially feel liberating. This can be especially true for individuals who struggle with social anxiety in real-life settings. However, this very anonymity can also create a barrier to authentic connection. Overcoming this hurdle often involves intentional self-disclosure, starting with small, manageable steps. Sharing personal interests within relevant online communities, participating in group activities, and engaging in respectful conversations can gradually build trust and foster meaningful relationships. Remember, vulnerability is key; showing your true self, even in a digital space, is a powerful way to connect with others.

Don't underestimate the power of shared experiences. Collaborating on projects, participating in virtual events, or simply enjoying the same game can create a strong sense of camaraderie and shared identity. These shared experiences forge bonds that transcend the digital divide, fostering genuine friendships and support systems. Look for groups and communities aligned with your interests; passionate individuals are often eager to connect with like-minded peers.

The feeling of belonging is fundamental to human well-being. In virtual worlds, this can be achieved through active participation in online communities. Contributing to discussions, offering help to others, and demonstrating empathy are all crucial for building a sense of belonging and reciprocity. Seek out supportive communities that prioritize positive interaction and mutual respect. Avoid spaces known for negativity or toxicity; your well-being is paramount.

However, the ease of online interaction shouldn't overshadow the importance of offline connections. Balancing your virtual and real-world relationships is vital. Remember, technology is a tool to enhance, not replace, genuine human connections. Make time for both your digital and real-life social circles, ensuring that neither is neglected. A well-rounded social life, incorporating both virtual and physical interactions, generally promotes a healthier sense of balance and well-being.

Remember that not all online communities are created equal. Some may foster a sense of inclusion and support, while others may be toxic and harmful. If you find yourself in a negative or unsupportive online environment, don't hesitate to leave. Your mental and emotional health are far more important than any virtual community. Seek out spaces that prioritize respect, empathy, and genuine connection. It's crucial to prioritize your well-being and choose environments that nurture your mental health.

5 Community & Connection Online

One effective strategy for fostering a sense of belonging is to actively contribute to the community. This could involve participating in discussions, sharing your knowledge and expertise, mentoring newcomers, or organizing events. By actively participating, you not only build relationships but also contribute to a positive and supportive environment for others. This reciprocal exchange strengthens the bonds within the community, reinforcing a sense of belonging and shared purpose. This active engagement also helps to cultivate a feeling of ownership and investment in the community's success.

Maintaining a healthy balance between your online and offline life is crucial for preventing feelings of isolation and maintaining a well-rounded social life. This involves setting boundaries for your time spent online and consciously making time for real-world interactions. Prioritize face-to-face interactions with loved ones and participate in activities that connect you with your local community. This balance ensures that your virtual world interactions enrich your life, rather than replace vital offline connections. Remember that genuine connections, regardless of their medium, are vital for well-being.

Furthermore, it is important to cultivate self-awareness regarding your online behavior. Reflect on your interactions and assess whether they align with your values and promote positive relationships. If you find yourself engaging in behavior that is harmful or unconstructive, take a step back and reassess your approach. This self-reflection is crucial for maintaining healthy relationships in the virtual world. Actively cultivate self-compassion and recognize that making mistakes online is part of the learning process.

Finally, remember that building strong relationships takes time and effort, both online and offline. Be patient, persistent, and respectful in your interactions. Authentic connections are built on mutual trust, respect, and shared experiences. While virtual worlds offer unique opportunities for connection, it's crucial to approach them with intentionality and self-awareness. Prioritize building relationships with people who genuinely care about you and support your growth, both in the virtual and real world.

5.3 Combatting Online Isolation

Feeling disconnected? Loneliness in the digital age isn't a sign of failure; it's a common experience, amplified by the very technologies meant to connect us. The vibrant online communities depicted in science fiction often feel a world away from the reality of sporadic interactions and superficial connections. Don't let the illusion of constant connectivity fool you; genuine connection requires effort, even—perhaps especially—online.

Finding your tribe online takes intentionality. Avoid passively scrolling; actively seek out communities aligned with your interests. Join online forums, participate in discussions, and contribute meaningfully. Remember, online communities thrive on reciprocal engagement. Sharing your thoughts and experiences fosters a sense of belonging, while actively listening to others builds genuine relationships. Don't just lurk; become an active member.

Consider the nature of your online interactions. Superficial likes and comments offer little emotional sustenance. Seek out platforms that encourage deeper engagement, where meaningful conversations can unfold. Prioritize quality over quantity; a few genuine connections are far more valuable than hundreds of fleeting interactions. Focus on building relationships with individuals who share your values and

5 Community & Connection Online

support your personal growth.

Vulnerability is key to forming authentic connections. Sharing personal experiences, even online, can be incredibly powerful. It creates a space for empathy and understanding, fostering a deeper sense of connection with others. This doesn't mean oversharing; it's about sharing selectively, with people you trust, in a way that feels comfortable and safe. Remember to assess your comfort level and the online environment before sharing something personal.

Combatting isolation also means actively managing your online time. Excessive screen time can exacerbate feelings of loneliness. Set healthy boundaries, scheduling specific times for online interactions and ensuring you dedicate time to offline activities that nourish your well-being. Balance your virtual life with real-world connections; cultivate relationships with friends and family, engaging in activities that foster in-person interaction.

Remember, online communities are only one piece of the puzzle. Your well-being extends beyond the digital realm. Make an effort to nurture relationships offline. Engage in hobbies and activities that bring you joy, and make time for face-to-face interactions with loved ones. These offline experiences contribute to a sense of wholeness that online interactions, no matter how positive, cannot entirely replicate.

Don't hesitate to seek professional support if you're struggling with online isolation or other mental health challenges. Therapists can provide guidance and tools to help you navigate these feelings and build healthier online and offline relationships. Many therapists now offer online sessions, making it easier to access support regardless of location or scheduling constraints. Reaching out for help is a sign of strength, not weakness.

5.3 Combatting Online Isolation

Cultivating meaningful connections, online or offline, takes time and effort. Be patient with yourself, and celebrate small victories along the way. Building strong relationships takes time, and fostering genuine connections requires consistent effort and self-awareness. Remember that forming meaningful connections—even online—is a process, not a destination.

Finally, remember the power of self-compassion. It's easy to compare yourself to others online, especially in curated digital spaces. Focus on your strengths and celebrate your achievements. Remember that online representations rarely reflect the full complexity of a person's life. Practice self-kindness, acknowledging your feelings without judgment and seeking support when needed. Your journey toward overcoming online isolation is a personal one, and it's important to be kind to yourself throughout the process. Be patient, be persistent, and remember that you are not alone in this.

6 The Dark Side of Virtual Worlds

Excessive immersion in virtual worlds can lead to a concerning level of addiction, mirroring the addictive nature of other compulsive behaviors. The dopamine rush associated with achieving goals, leveling up, or social interaction within these environments can create a powerful feedback loop, making it difficult to disengage. This can manifest as neglecting real-life responsibilities, strained relationships, and a decline in physical and mental health. Individuals may experience withdrawal symptoms upon attempting to reduce their virtual engagement, further solidifying the addictive cycle. The allure of escape, immediate gratification, and readily available rewards makes it a significant challenge to break free, highlighting the importance of preventative measures and early intervention strategies. Recognizing the warning signs is crucial for both individuals and their support networks, as it's often a gradual descent into excessive use that may not be apparent until significant consequences have already manifested. The blurring of lines between the virtual and real world can be particularly insidious, gradually eroding the sense of balance necessary for a healthy life.

6 The Dark Side of Virtual Worlds

Cyberbullying and harassment in virtual worlds pose a significant threat to mental well-being. Unlike physical interactions, online interactions lack the immediate nonverbal cues that help regulate social encounters. The anonymity offered by many online platforms emboldens some to engage in aggressive and abusive behavior without facing immediate consequences. This can lead to significant psychological distress, including anxiety, depression, low self-esteem, and even suicidal ideation, particularly among vulnerable individuals. The pervasive nature of online interactions means that victims may experience harassment persistently and across multiple platforms. The lack of physical boundaries in the virtual space exacerbates the impact, as the digital harassment can feel inescapable and incredibly personal. Effective moderation and reporting mechanisms are critical, yet the sheer scale of online interactions makes complete eradication an insurmountable challenge. Building resilience in young users and promoting empathy and responsible online behavior are crucial preventative strategies.

The risks to mental health extend beyond addiction and cyberbullying. Prolonged exposure to virtual environments can negatively impact sleep patterns, social skills, and physical health. The immersive nature of these spaces can lead to feelings of isolation and detachment from real-life relationships. Individuals may struggle to differentiate between their virtual and real-life identities, potentially leading to identity confusion and issues with self-esteem. Furthermore, the curated nature of virtual worlds can create unrealistic expectations about appearance, achievement, and social success. This constant comparison can contribute to feelings of inadequacy and anxiety. The lack of physical activity associated with prolonged virtual immersion contributes to a sedentary lifestyle, leading to various health problems.

While virtual reality offers therapeutic potential, its responsible use is critical to avoid compounding existing mental health challenges. Promoting mental wellbeing involves understanding the potential risks, educating users, and providing appropriate support systems.

Maintaining a healthy balance between virtual and real-life interactions is crucial for mitigating the potential negative consequences. This involves setting clear boundaries on the time spent in virtual worlds, actively engaging in real-life activities, nurturing real-world relationships, and fostering self-awareness around one's virtual engagement habits. Practicing mindfulness and cultivating self-regulation skills can help individuals manage their impulses and resist the urge to over-immerse themselves. Establishing a structured routine that integrates both virtual and real-life activities allows for a more balanced lifestyle. Furthermore, seeking support from friends, family, or mental health professionals can be beneficial for those struggling to manage their virtual world engagement. Encouraging open communication and creating a non-judgmental environment for discussing these challenges helps destigmatize seeking help and facilitates positive change. Ultimately, the key lies in utilizing virtual worlds as a tool for personal growth, rather than allowing them to dominate and negatively impact one's life. This requires conscious effort, self-reflection, and a commitment to prioritize well-being in both the virtual and real worlds.

6.1 Addiction & Virtual Reality

The allure of virtual reality (VR) is undeniable; immersive worlds beckon with the promise of escape and adventure. Yet, this very allure can be a pathway to addiction, a slippery slope that gradually shifts priorities and erodes real-life connections. For many, the line between

6 The Dark Side of Virtual Worlds

healthy engagement and problematic use blurs subtly, starting with extended play sessions that slowly morph into all-consuming habits. The immediate gratification offered by VR games, social interactions, and even simulated experiences can hijack the brain's reward system, leading to compulsive behavior. This is further exacerbated by the ease of access and the constantly evolving nature of VR technology, which offers a seemingly endless stream of new and captivating content.

Unlike substance addiction, where physical withdrawal symptoms might be prominent, VR addiction manifests differently. It's characterized by a profound sense of withdrawal, marked by irritability, anxiety, and intense cravings when access is limited. Individuals might neglect their responsibilities, jeopardizing relationships, academic pursuits, or careers, all in a desperate attempt to escape into the virtual realm. The isolation that can accompany excessive VR use often worsens existing mental health challenges or triggers new ones. The constant stimulation and the artificial nature of these experiences can disrupt sleep patterns, leading to fatigue and reduced cognitive function.

Recognizing the signs of VR addiction is crucial for both individuals and their support systems. Changes in behavior, such as withdrawal from social activities, neglecting personal hygiene, and significant reductions in sleep, should trigger concern. Increased irritability, decreased motivation, and a pervasive sense of guilt or shame further point towards a potential problem. Financial difficulties stemming from excessive spending on VR equipment or in-game purchases also serve as red flags. Remember, addiction is a spectrum, and early intervention is key.

Seeking professional help is a crucial step in overcoming VR addiction. Therapists specializing in behavioral addictions can offer guidance and

6.1 Addiction & Virtual Reality

support through various therapeutic approaches. Cognitive Behavioral Therapy (CBT), for example, can help individuals identify and challenge the negative thought patterns and behaviors contributing to their addiction. Motivational interviewing, another effective technique, focuses on fostering intrinsic motivation for change, empowering individuals to take control of their habits. Support groups, either online or in person, offer a sense of community and shared experience, allowing individuals to connect with others facing similar challenges. These groups provide a safe space to share experiences, learn coping strategies, and gain valuable support.

Beyond professional intervention, building a strong support network is fundamental. Open communication with family and friends is vital; letting loved ones know about the struggle allows them to offer practical assistance and understanding. Engaging in alternative activities that provide similar levels of engagement and satisfaction, but without the addictive element, can help to divert attention and create healthy alternatives. This might involve rediscovering hobbies, reconnecting with old friends, joining sports teams, or pursuing creative endeavors. It's important to find activities that provide genuine fulfillment and a sense of accomplishment, helping to replace the artificial gratification of virtual worlds.

Furthermore, establishing clear boundaries around VR usage is crucial. Setting time limits, designating specific times for VR sessions, and creating clear consequences for exceeding these limits can help to regain control. This structured approach provides a framework for managing VR usage, preventing it from spiraling into uncontrolled consumption. Regularly evaluating one's usage patterns and honestly reflecting on the impact of VR on various aspects of life—work, relationships, and overall well-being—is an important tool for self-regulation. Building self-awareness is essential to identify early warning signs and prevent relapses.

In conclusion, while virtual reality offers an array of engaging experiences and opportunities, it's crucial to maintain a healthy balance. Recognizing the potential for addiction and implementing proactive strategies for prevention and intervention is paramount. Open communication, professional guidance, and the development of alternative, fulfilling activities are key components in mitigating the risks associated with excessive VR use and promoting a healthier relationship with technology. Remembering that recovery is a journey, not a destination, fosters patience and resilience, fostering long-term success. The path to a balanced and fulfilling life often involves navigating the complexities of technology, learning to harness its potential while maintaining a strong connection to the real world.

6.2 Cyberbullying & Harassment

The anonymity offered by the internet, a seemingly liberating force, can unfortunately foster a breeding ground for cruelty. Cyberbullying and harassment, unlike their real-world counterparts, often lack the immediate constraints of physical presence. This digital distance emboldens perpetrators, allowing them to inflict emotional damage with a chilling detachment. Victims, often feeling isolated and helpless, can suffer profound psychological distress, impacting their self-esteem, academic performance, and overall well-being. The insidious nature of online harassment, its potential for widespread dissemination, and its enduring impact demand careful consideration.

Understanding the dynamics of cyberbullying is crucial to effectively

6.2 Cyberbullying & Harassment

addressing it. It's not just about isolated incidents; it's a complex pattern of behavior, often involving repeated attacks, intimidation, and exclusion. These attacks can manifest in various forms: harassing messages, threats, public shaming, doxxing (the release of personal information), or even the creation of fake profiles designed to spread malicious rumors. The persistent nature of online content further exacerbates the problem, leaving a digital trail of abuse that can haunt victims for years. This enduring presence intensifies the emotional burden, making it harder to escape the cycle of harassment.

Prevention is paramount. Educating young people about online safety and responsible digital citizenship is not merely a good idea; it's a necessity. This includes teaching them to identify different forms of online harassment, understand the potential consequences of their actions, and develop strategies for self-protection. Open communication within families and schools is vital, fostering an environment where children feel comfortable reporting incidents without fear of judgment or retribution. Creating a culture of empathy and respect, both online and offline, is a long-term investment in a safer digital landscape.

Moreover, fostering resilience in potential victims is equally critical. Equipping individuals with coping mechanisms and emotional regulation techniques helps them navigate the challenges of online harassment. Building strong support networks, both online and offline, allows them to lean on trusted individuals during difficult times. This involves encouraging active participation in supportive online communities that promote positive interactions and discourage harmful behavior. Remember, social support acts as a crucial buffer against the negative impacts of cyberbullying.

Platforms themselves bear a significant responsibility. They must proactively implement robust reporting mechanisms, promptly address complaints, and take decisive action against perpetrators. This necessitates investing in advanced technology to detect and prevent harassment, as well as developing clearer policies and enforcement procedures. Transparency in their actions and a commitment to user safety are crucial for fostering trust and accountability. The creation of safer online spaces requires a collaborative effort between users, educators, and platform providers.

The legal landscape surrounding cyberbullying is constantly evolving. Laws vary across jurisdictions, and enforcement can be challenging given the global nature of the internet. Nonetheless, understanding existing legal frameworks and exploring avenues for redress is crucial for victims seeking recourse. Knowing their rights and the steps they can take to seek justice empowers them to take control of the situation and potentially prevent future incidents. This legal awareness, combined with strong emotional support, can dramatically improve a victim's ability to recover and regain their sense of security.

Finally, remember that recovery from cyberbullying is a journey, not a destination. It involves a process of healing, self-discovery, and the rebuilding of trust. Seeking professional help from therapists or counselors specializing in trauma and cyberbullying is often vital. These professionals can provide the necessary support and guidance to help victims process their experiences, develop coping strategies, and ultimately regain a sense of well-being. The path to recovery requires patience, understanding, and a dedicated commitment to self-care. Cyberbullying leaves deep scars, but with the right support and intervention, recovery and resilience are absolutely possible.

6.3 Mental Health Risks

Excessive immersion in virtual worlds can lead to several mental health concerns. Prolonged exposure, particularly to violent or stressful virtual content, may trigger anxiety, depression, or even exacerbate pre-existing conditions. The blurring of lines between the virtual and real can contribute to feelings of detachment from reality, impacting social skills and real-world relationships. For individuals already struggling with mental health, virtual worlds can become an escape, potentially delaying or hindering necessary treatment and support. This isn't to say that virtual worlds are inherently negative; rather, it underscores the crucial need for mindful engagement and awareness of potential risks.

Understanding the potential for addiction is paramount. The immersive nature of virtual environments, coupled with rewarding game mechanics or social interactions, can lead to compulsive usage. This excessive engagement can disrupt sleep patterns, neglecting real-life responsibilities, impacting academic or professional performance, and ultimately leading to social isolation and further mental health distress. Identifying the signs of addiction, such as neglecting personal hygiene, withdrawing from social activities, prioritizing virtual interactions over real-life commitments, and experiencing withdrawal symptoms upon disengagement, is crucial for early intervention. Seeking professional help is advisable if these symptoms are present.

Cyberbullying and online harassment represent a significant mental health risk within virtual environments. The anonymity afforded by virtual platforms can embolden negative behaviors, leading to targeted harassment, social exclusion, and significant emotional distress. The persistent nature of online interactions exacerbates the impact of

6 The Dark Side of Virtual Worlds

such incidents, potentially leading to feelings of helplessness, low self-esteem, and anxiety. It's vital to recognize the long-term effects of this type of abuse on mental wellbeing. Early intervention, support networks, and reporting mechanisms can help mitigate the damage.

The constant comparison with idealized avatars and the pressure to maintain a perfect virtual persona can significantly impact self-esteem and body image. The curated nature of virtual identities often presents an unrealistic standard of beauty and success. This can lead to feelings of inadequacy, anxiety about one's own appearance, and even contribute to the development of body dysmorphia, especially in vulnerable individuals. Promoting healthy self-perception and encouraging realistic expectations are crucial. Emphasizing self-acceptance and understanding the performative nature of online presentations are essential strategies to navigate these challenges successfully.

Furthermore, the lack of non-verbal cues in digital communication can lead to misinterpretations and conflicts, potentially fueling anxiety and impacting the quality of virtual relationships. The absence of physical touch and immediate feedback can make virtual interactions feel less meaningful, leading to feelings of loneliness and isolation, even within a seemingly active online community. Developing strong communication skills and practicing empathy are essential tools to foster healthier online interactions, mitigating potential negative impacts on mental well-being. Active participation in offline activities and prioritizing real-world connections can also help counterbalance these potential downsides.

Another concern is the impact of virtual worlds on sleep quality and circadian rhythm. The stimulating nature of virtual environments, often associated with late-night gaming sessions or prolonged virtual interaction, can disrupt sleep patterns, leading to fatigue, irritability, and impaired cognitive function. Chronic sleep deprivation is detrimental to mental health, increasing vulnerability to depression, anxiety, and other mental health problems. Establishing healthy sleep hygiene, limiting screen time before bed, and ensuring adequate rest are crucial for maintaining mental wellbeing within the context of virtual world engagement.

Finally, recognizing the impact of virtual environments on individuals with pre-existing mental health conditions is crucial. Virtual worlds can act as both a trigger and a coping mechanism, depending on individual circumstances and the nature of the virtual experience. For example, individuals with social anxiety may find online interactions less daunting, potentially leading to improved social skills and increased self-confidence. Conversely, the same environments could heighten anxiety levels if faced with aggressive or overwhelming virtual experiences. A nuanced understanding of the individual's mental health landscape is crucial when considering their engagement with virtual worlds. Professional guidance is vital in navigating this complex interaction.

6.4 Balancing Virtual & Real Life

The allure of virtual worlds is undeniable; the vibrant landscapes, the engaging narratives, the limitless possibilities. It's easy to get lost in the immersive experiences they offer, to prioritize the digital over the tangible. But neglecting your real life while engrossed in virtual ones can lead to a precarious imbalance. This isn't about demonizing virtual environments – far from it. Instead, it's about fostering a healthy relationship with them, one that enriches your life without overshadowing it.

Maintaining this balance requires conscious effort and a clear understanding of your priorities. Ask yourself: what brings you joy and fulfillment in the real world? Are there activities you've neglected due to excessive time spent online? Reconnecting with those activities, whether it's spending time with loved ones, pursuing a hobby, or simply enjoying nature, is crucial. Make a schedule; allocate specific time slots for online activities and stick to them as rigorously as you would any important appointment.

Remember the feeling of accomplishment after completing a challenging task in a game? This sense of achievement is transferable to the real world. Set realistic goals for yourself, both online and offline. Break down larger projects into smaller, manageable steps to avoid feeling overwhelmed. Celebrate your successes, no matter how small, acknowledging your progress in both virtual and real-life endeavors. This fosters a sense of consistent growth and well-being.

Social interaction plays a vital role in our well-being, both online and offline. While virtual communities can offer support and connection, they shouldn't replace real-world relationships. Make an effort to nurture your relationships with friends and family. Schedule regular phone calls, video chats, or in-person meetings. Prioritize quality time over quantity, focusing on meaningful connections rather than superficial interactions.

Maintaining a healthy sleep schedule is paramount. The blue light emitted from screens can disrupt your circadian rhythm, impacting your sleep quality. Establish a consistent sleep routine, avoiding screen time at least an hour before bed. Create a relaxing bedtime ritual to help you unwind and prepare for sleep. Prioritize sleep; it's essential

6.4 Balancing Virtual & Real Life

for both your physical and mental health, regardless of your virtual escapades.

Physical health often takes a backseat when we're engrossed in virtual worlds. Prolonged periods of inactivity can lead to a range of health problems. Incorporate regular exercise into your daily routine. Even short bursts of activity throughout the day can make a difference. Find activities you enjoy, whether it's a brisk walk, a cycling trip, or a gym workout. Remember that physical health is interconnected with mental well-being; neglecting one will inevitably affect the other.

Many individuals find mindfulness practices beneficial in managing stress and improving overall well-being. These techniques can be applied to both virtual and real life. Engage in activities that promote mindfulness, such as meditation or yoga, to help you stay grounded and present in your daily life. Practice mindful gaming, focusing on the present moment and appreciating the experience rather than becoming overly competitive or emotionally invested.

Consider your digital footprint and the information you share online. Protecting your privacy and mental health online requires awareness and responsible behavior. Be mindful of what you share and who you interact with. Engage in healthy online habits and report any instances of cyberbullying or harassment. Remember, online interactions can leave a lasting impression, so maintaining responsible digital conduct is crucial for your overall well-being.

Finally, remember that balance is not a static state but a dynamic process. Your needs and priorities will change over time, and so will your relationship with virtual worlds. Regularly evaluate your online habits and adjust accordingly. If you find yourself spending excessive time online, take a step back and re-evaluate your priorities. Seek professional help if needed. Remember that seeking support is a sign of strength, not weakness, and crucial for maintaining a balanced life. A fulfilling life requires a harmonious integration of the real and the virtual, where both enhance, rather than detract from, your overall well-being.

7 Conclusion: Shaping the Future

The convergence of virtual and augmented realities promises a future brimming with unprecedented possibilities. Imagine a world where personalized therapeutic interventions are delivered seamlessly through immersive VR experiences, tailored to individual needs and preferences, resulting in a wider accessibility of mental health support and a significant reduction in the stigma associated with seeking professional help. The development of sophisticated AI-driven systems could analyze user interactions within these virtual environments, providing real-time feedback and adaptive treatments, enhancing the effectiveness and personalization of therapeutic approaches.

Beyond therapy, educational applications will flourish. Imagine students exploring historical sites or dissecting complex biological systems, all within the safety and control of a virtual setting. The limitations of traditional classrooms will melt away, replaced by immersive, interactive learning experiences. This personalized approach, catering to diverse learning styles and paces, will foster a deeper understanding and engagement with educational material, ultimately leading to improved learning outcomes. The potential for global collaboration

7 Conclusion: Shaping the Future

will also grow exponentially, facilitating cross-cultural exchange and creating a truly connected global learning community.

However, the journey toward this optimistic future requires mindful navigation. The ethical implications of pervasive virtual environments demand careful consideration. Data privacy, algorithmic bias, and the potential for manipulation must be addressed proactively. Responsible design principles, prioritizing user well-being and safety, need to be at the forefront of all development efforts. This includes creating clear guidelines and safety nets to mitigate the risk of addiction, cyberbullying, and other negative consequences associated with prolonged virtual world engagement. Transparency and user control over their data are paramount.

Furthermore, addressing the digital divide is crucial. Equitable access to VR/AR technologies is essential to ensure that the benefits of these innovations are shared by all members of society. Strategies to bridge the gap between those with access and those without must be implemented to prevent further societal stratification. We must actively promote digital literacy and equip individuals with the tools and skills needed to navigate the virtual world safely and responsibly. Focusing on education and public awareness campaigns targeting various demographic groups can help level the playing field.

The creation of robust regulatory frameworks is also essential. Collaboration between policymakers, technology developers, and mental health professionals is vital to establish standards that safeguard user safety and protect vulnerable populations. This collaborative effort should strive for a balanced approach that encourages innovation while mitigating potential risks. This would involve setting clear standards for data privacy, content moderation, and the responsible use of virtual environments, helping prevent misuse and harm.

Ultimately, shaping the future of VR/AR requires a collective commitment to responsible innovation and ethical considerations. It necessitates a proactive approach to addressing potential challenges and a collaborative effort to harness the transformative power of these technologies for the betterment of humanity. By prioritizing user well-being, promoting inclusivity, and fostering a culture of responsible development, we can unlock the extraordinary potential of virtual and augmented realities to enrich human lives and drive positive societal transformation. The future is not simply a technological advancement; it's a shared responsibility, requiring a continuous dialogue between creators and users to ensure its positive impact. Failure to address these critical aspects could lead to a future where the promise of these technologies remains unfulfilled, overshadowed by unforeseen consequences. The potential for good is immense, but it hinges on our collective dedication to shaping a responsible and inclusive virtual world.

7.1 Future Trends in VR/AR

Haptic feedback will become increasingly sophisticated, moving beyond simple vibrations to more nuanced sensations. Imagine feeling the texture of a virtual object, the warmth of a virtual sun, or even the resistance of a virtual tool. This will profoundly impact VR therapy, allowing for more immersive and effective treatments for phobias and other conditions. Consider the possibilities for surgical training – surgeons could practice complex procedures on virtual patients with lifelike tactile responses, improving precision and minimizing risks in real-world surgeries. The enhanced realism will also boost engagement in educational VR experiences, making learning more interactive

7 Conclusion: Shaping the Future

and memorable. We can anticipate a rise in specialized haptic devices tailored to specific applications, from gaming controllers offering realistic weapon recoil to medical simulators providing the exact feel of human tissues. This evolution will not only enhance entertainment and training, but will also significantly contribute to advancements in fields like healthcare and engineering.

The integration of artificial intelligence (AI) will redefine VR and AR experiences. AI-powered NPCs (non-player characters) will behave more naturally, reacting dynamically to user actions and displaying more complex emotions and motivations. This increased realism will greatly enrich gaming and virtual social environments, offering more engaging and believable interactions. AI algorithms can also personalize user experiences by adapting game difficulty, storyline, or even the virtual environment itself to individual preferences. Furthermore, AI could play a pivotal role in creating hyper-realistic virtual worlds, generating detailed and expansive landscapes without relying on extensive manual design. Think of breathtaking virtual cities that seamlessly blend realistic architecture with fantastical elements, generated and rendered in real-time by AI. The future holds endless possibilities for AI-driven content creation in VR/AR environments, leading to unparalleled levels of immersion and personalization.

Augmented reality (AR) will become more seamlessly integrated into our daily lives. We are already seeing this with AR navigation apps and filters on social media platforms. However, the future of AR will involve more sophisticated overlays that are more context-aware and less intrusive. Imagine an AR application that provides real-time information about a historical landmark as you view it, or an AR overlay that guides you through a complex assembly process by highlight-

7.1 Future Trends in VR/AR

ing relevant parts of the object you are working on. The development of lightweight, stylish AR glasses will make it more convenient and socially acceptable to wear AR devices throughout the day. We can envision a future where AR glasses provide unobtrusive notifications, translate languages in real-time, or even enhance our perception of the world by highlighting points of interest or providing relevant information. This increased integration of AR into our everyday routines will lead to a more efficient, informative, and potentially more enriching experience of the world around us.

The metaverse will continue to evolve, moving beyond simple gaming environments to more complex and integrated virtual worlds. Interoperability will become a key factor, allowing users to seamlessly transition between different metaverse platforms and retain their identities and assets. We'll see greater integration of different forms of digital assets, virtual currencies and NFTs (non-fungible tokens), which will create new opportunities for creators, businesses, and users within these virtual ecosystems. The establishment of clearer legal frameworks and standards is crucial to encourage responsible development and foster user trust within these digital spaces. Increased emphasis will be placed on fostering genuine community and a sense of belonging within the metaverse. This could involve developing more robust social mechanisms, encouraging collaborative experiences, and promoting positive social interactions within the virtual environment. The metaverse, in its fully realized form, will transcend mere entertainment to become a new realm of social interaction, commerce, and creation.

Accessibility will become a key focus in VR/AR development. We can expect advancements in technologies such as adaptive controllers, eye-tracking systems, and brain-computer interfaces that make VR and AR experiences accessible to people with disabilities. These advancements will empower individuals with diverse needs, opening up new opportunities for education, therapy, and social interaction. There will also be a growing emphasis on the design of inclusivity, ensuring that virtual worlds reflect the diversity of the real world and cater to the needs of all users. This includes representing different cultures, backgrounds, and physical abilities, fostering inclusivity in virtual environments, and building a more accepting and representative digital society. The expansion of accessibility will bring in a wider audience for VR/AR, enabling more people to benefit from these transformative technologies.

7.2 Responsible Virtual World Design

Designing responsible virtual worlds demands a proactive approach, prioritizing user well-being above all else. We must move beyond simply creating immersive environments and instead focus on crafting spaces that nurture mental health and foster positive social interactions. This requires a multi-faceted strategy, addressing issues from the initial design phase through to ongoing monitoring and community management.

The architecture of a virtual world profoundly impacts user experience. Consider the layout, navigation, and overall aesthetic. A confusing or overwhelming design can induce anxiety, while a calming and intuitive environment can promote relaxation and focus. For instance, incorporating natural elements like virtual plants and calming soundscapes can create a sense of peace, reducing stress levels within the digital space. Similarly, clear pathways and intuitive interfaces minimize frustration and enhance user experience. These seemingly minor

7.2 Responsible Virtual World Design

details significantly contribute to the overall feeling of safety and well-being.

Beyond aesthetics, the social dynamics within a virtual world require careful consideration. Robust anti-harassment and anti-bullying systems are paramount. These shouldn't be afterthoughts, but integral design elements implemented from the ground up. Real-time monitoring and swift responses to reported incidents are crucial. Furthermore, community building features that encourage positive interactions, such as collaborative projects or shared experiences, are vital for combating feelings of isolation and fostering a sense of belonging. These features should actively promote connection and cooperation rather than just competition.

Inclusivity is another critical aspect. Responsible design necessitates accessibility for users of all abilities. This involves careful consideration of visual and auditory impairments, motor skill limitations, and diverse cultural backgrounds. Clear communication options, adjustable settings, and diverse avatar customization options ensure a welcoming environment for everyone. Failing to account for such diversities can exclude significant portions of the population, negating the potential benefits of virtual worlds for all.

Data privacy is a concern that demands clear and transparent policies. Users must understand how their data is collected, used, and protected. This involves not only adhering to relevant regulations but also building trust through clear and accessible privacy statements and consistent practices. Transparency and user control are pivotal in mitigating risks and building confidence. Users must feel empowered to manage their personal information within the virtual world.

Furthermore, developers need to consider the potential for addiction.

7 Conclusion: Shaping the Future

Game mechanics should be designed to prevent compulsive behavior. This could involve implementing clear time limits, encouraging breaks, and providing easy access to resources on responsible use. Integration of well-being prompts and educational materials about healthy digital habits directly within the virtual world can help users maintain a balanced approach to their virtual engagements.

Finally, ongoing evaluation and adaptation are essential. Regular user feedback, combined with data analysis, allows for continuous improvement. Identifying areas for improvement and responding proactively is key to maintaining a safe and positive environment. This iterative approach, constantly refining design and policies based on real-world usage and feedback, will ensure the virtual world evolves to meet the needs of its users and reflect a responsible and ethical commitment to well-being. This is not merely a matter of compliance but a fundamental principle underpinning the creation of genuinely beneficial virtual experiences. The long-term success of any virtual world hinges on this commitment to responsible design.

www.ingramcontent.com/pod-product-compliance
Lightning Source LLC
LaVergne TN
LVHW012035060526
838201LV00061B/4612